Contents

Lairy hair   2

Mrs Fairborn's baby   6

What sort of football fan are you - fanatical,
fair or a flop?   10

It's football - but not as we know it!   14

Norman Knight, time-travelling superstar   18

Christmas 1914   22

Troy Tomato cooks up a storm   26

Unwrap - and enjoy!   30

Room rage!   34

Get your skates on!   39

Green words, Red words, Challenge words
and vocabulary check   44

Lairy hair

So a trip to the hairdressers is bliss, right? A cut every 6 weeks to keep the cool look? Or is your fantasy that one day you might be hairdresser to pop and film stars? Snipping away at Posh's locks and brushing Beckham's barnet! Well, think some more, as hair has a flair for being a bit, you might say … lairy, and it doesn't always play fair.

Get this – you think you are a hairdresser "extraordinaire". There is a customer in the salon chair. They show you a pop star in a mag and say they need to look as good as that.

You wash the hair.
You trim the hair.
It does not look good.
You snip a bit more … and more … and more. The customer's hair does not match the pop star's hair yet. The air is full of hair and you are full of despair.

Oops!

Problem is you have gone too far – ever had a go at repairing hair? Will hair do what you want? No way! Hair will not play fair! You end up giving the customer their money back. Well, you can't give the hair back, can you?

And what happens when you get asked to do a mad haircut? You can't hoot and snort when a lad pops in and asks for a cut that looks as if it was in fashion when your grandad as a kid!

There have been some bizarre haircuts in the past – one was called a mullet! Lots of football stars had this cut. The best known "mullet man" was a football star of the 70s, Kevin Keegan. Dads and lads rushed off to get the cool Keegan look.

Hair is so odd. Still want to spend days on end playing with hair?

Lairy hair facts

Lairy hair fact number 1

Hair is the fastest-growing tissue on your body!

OK, you might say, that's not so odd. Try this then ...

Lairy hair fact number 2

A loss of 100 hairs a day is normal!

Still not impressed?
Here is lairy hair fact number 3

A hair could hold the weight of a 100 gram choccy bar before snapping. Did you say boring? That's it then – you get the lairiest hair fact of all. This will shock you (get a chair).

Lairy hair fact number 4

An insect called a wood roach scoffs as much hair as it can.

Yuck! Yes, it's a fact. Hair has a chemical called keratin in it and that keeps the insect's shell strong!

But don't let me put you off. A hairdresser to the top stars can get as much as £700 for giving them a haircut! Now where did I put that hairbrush ...

Mrs Fairborn's baby

Mrs Rapunzel Fairborn had a lot to be thankful for. She had the long, golden hair that had always been in her family. She had a good husband, Mr Alistair Fairborn, and she had a job. She had to wash and sweep up hair in the top celebrity hair salon, 'Tumbling Tresses'.

But she adored children and longed for a child of her own to love.

"Do not despair!" said Mr Fairborn. "We will have a child one day and she will have your long, golden hair!"

One hectic day in the 'Tumbling Tresses' hair salon, a wizened old gran, with just a few strands of hair left on her bony skull, snuck in for a trim. She sat herself in the top celebrity sparkly chair. (It was only ever sat upon by celeb of celebs, DJ Cool Kat.) Rapunzel was sweeping up hair, the hairdressers were snipping, gelling and spraying and not one of them spotted her – oops!

A blast of cold air hit the salon and in swept DJ Cool Kat.

"Hair. Sort it. Pronto!" she bellowed.

Whipping off her dark glasses, Cool Kat click-clacked in her high heels to *her* chair. Then she let out the screech of a lost prairie dog. It hung in mid-air.

"What is that *thing* in *my* chair? Get up, you old fool!"

She had a flair for being fairly dramatic.

Mrs Rapunzel Fairborn had a soft spot not just for children, but for old folk too. She forgot who she was. She forgot the salon boss. She had seen Cool Kat being unfair before, but this was too much ... Rapunzel Fairborn flipped!

"Who do you think you are? Goldilocks? You haven't got the hair for it!" Rapunzel yelled. "You don't need a hairdo. You need some respect! This lady's staying in the celebrity chair!"

Well! Cool Kat fell off her high heels in shock. The salon boss didn't know if he wanted to sob or clap. But the old gran had something to say to Mrs Fairborn.

"You are strong and bold to stand up to such a bully. I want to repay you. Tell me, what do you and your husband wish for most of all?"

Maybe it wasn't magic, because this is no fairy story, but soon after, Ricky Alistair Patrick Unzel Fairborn was born with long (very long), golden hair. His mum sighed with bliss as old grans peeped into the pram and said, "All that golden hair! Isn't *she* sweet?"

Not even magic always gets it right ...

What sort of football fan are you – fanatical, fair or a flop?

Think you know? Check first in this fun football quiz!

1) A red card is

a) given when you have not played well.

b) shown when you will be sent off the pitch for being a dirty player.

c) what you get from a craft shop.

2) A penalty shoot-out is

a) when teams keep playing until there is a winner.

b) when the score is a draw and you need a winner, so players shoot at the net. First to score the most is the winner.

c) ... sounds a bit odd – is it to do with hunting?

3) The penalty spot is

a) a circle on the pitch that you stand on for a penalty kick.

b) the spot the ball is put on for a penalty kick.

c) what you get on the end of your nose in your teens.

4) If you hit the post, you

a) whirl and twirl in circles and then crash into the goal post.

b) try to score but the ball hits the goal post first.

c) do a very nasty thing to that man who brings the post.

5) The World Cup is

a) a cup for thirsty players to drink from.

b) what every footballer in the world is stirred up to win.

c) good to put daffodils in to brighten up the locker rooms.

6) Studs are

a) to do with boots but I don't know what they are for.

b) on the bottom of football boots to give players a firm grip on a slippy pitch.

c) ... I know this one — they are little gold things you put in your ears.

The referee has blown the whistle.
Tot up your scores. If you got:

Mostly As

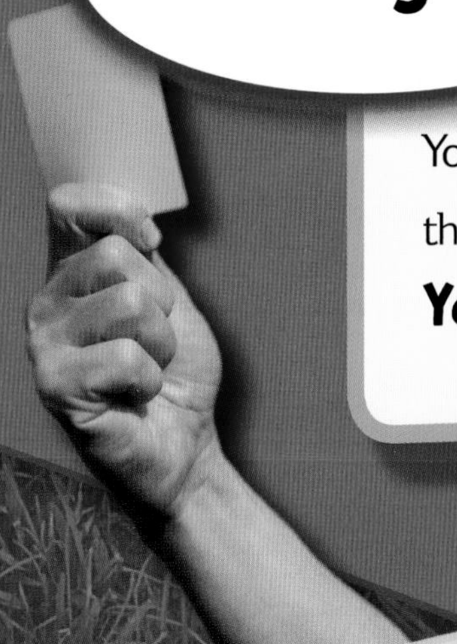

You know a bit of football stuff but you are still hitting the post. 3–0.

You are a fair football fan.

Mostly Bs

Right in the back of the net. Top score: 6–0.

You are a fanatical football fan.

Mostly Cs

I will try not to smirk. Do you know what a football is? You didn't get to kick-off. 0–0.

You are a flop of a football fan.

It's football –
but not as we know it!

Handball! Penalty! Yessss!

If you play football, it helps to understand the rules. Maybe you do (or think you do). But the rule book looked a lot different back in the 1860s ...

At first, each part of the country had its own set of firm rules. To be fair, they split each match in two, playing first by one team's set of rules, and then by the other. That's why matches today are still played in two halves.

Some rules from back then may seem a bit odd to us today ...

Teams must meet before the match to agree on:

- how long the pitch will be
- how long the match will last
- how many men will be on each team
- what sort of ball to play with.

A player may not pick the ball up, but he can catch the ball and run with it.

To shoot he must drop the ball first.

If a player is holding the ball, another player can kick him, grab at his shirt or strangle him!

A player may push the goalkeeper into the dirt.

Some dirty players might have spikes on the bottom of their boots. Ouch! This would stir the players up. Men had to be strong to play football. Women didn't play football until the 1900s.

You may not pass the ball forwards. As in rugby, you must pass to a man behind you.

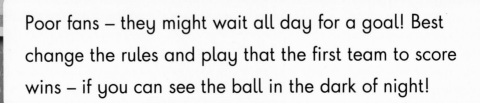

Poor fans – they might wait all day for a goal! Best change the rules and play that the first team to score wins – if you can see the ball in the dark of night!

Shirts shall have no names on them and may be any colour.

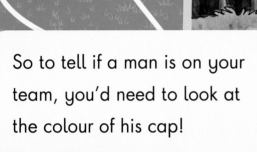

So to tell if a man is on your team, you'd need to look at the colour of his cap!

Two referees will be on the pitch, each twirling a flag. They must agree if a goal has been scored.

Goals have no nets, and maybe just string for a crossbar! The refs cannot send a player off, or even twirl their flags for a foul – players in the 1800s were too fair not to follow the rules. Just like today, right?

Norman Knight,
time-travelling superstar

Ashton Villa have got to their first FA Cup semi, one step away from Wembley, and are playing West Hum. But time is running out. Only one man can save them: Norman Knight, a player picked up from Stockport County (in 1895).

... and as we go into the last moments of this epic FA Cup semi, it looks as if Ashton Villa are about to go out. One–nil down, and with star player Rich Bird flat out on the ground after a bad foul. What do you think, Ray? Is Villa's proud Cup run about to end?

It looks that way, Alan.

But hang on, is that time-travelling superstar Norman Knight I see about to come on the pitch, Ray?

Yes, I think so, Alan.

He's putting his book down (after putting his bookmark in), finishing his beef sandwich and stepping out on to the pitch. What an odd sight he is, with his slick hair, black tash, long shorts, wooden shinpads and army boots.

Very odd, Alan.

He's got the ball now and is dribbling rings round the defence. He shoots ... the ball hits Bashford's hand ... penalty! And Bashford is sent off!

Norman Knight has won a penalty in the last seconds of the match. But what's going on? Norman's angry. He's telling the ref off! "Nonsense!" he's saying, "It's not a penalty! That's unfair!" But the ref is in no doubt. It is a penalty, and Knight will take it himself. Astonishing! What do you think, Ray?

It's astonishing, Alan.

But what's Norman doing? He seems to be saying sorry to the goalie. He's patting him on the back and wishing him luck. Now he's looking away from the goal. He's shooting at the corner flag! Astounding! Norman Knight has kicked the ball at the corner flag. Ray?

Astounding, Alan.

There isn't a sound round the ground. Sixty thousand fans are stunned. But the match has started again, and with just seconds to go Villa are on the attack. The ball is bouncing about by the West Hum goal. Knight pounces and sends it crashing into the back of the net. That's it! It's the end of the game! The West Hum men are on their knees. The Villa lads are jumping on Knight, men are trying to hug him and kiss him, but he's pushing them off. What's he saying, Ray?

He's telling them to be men, not silly infants, Alan. He's telling them to show respect for the West Hum lads and help them off the ground.

Astonishing. He's asking them to say thanks to the ref! And now the Villa fans are chanting: "One Norman Knight! There's only one Norman Knight!"

They are right there, Alan!

Christmas 1914

In 1914, Britain was at war with Germany. They were fighting in France. They fought from trenches with land in the middle known as no man's land. This letter, from a man who was there on Christmas Day 1914, shows an account of the first Christmas of the war.

27th December 1914

France

Dearest Father,

As your son, I wish I could have spent Christmas with you and Mother in our old house back in England, but as a soldier, I was proud to be with my Tommy pals. Today there has been a lot of shelling from the Germans and I should be snatching a bit of sleep, but I am scribbling this by candlelight as I sit in my cold dug-out. I want to tell you about the astonishing events of Christmas Day in the middle of no man's land.

It was a freezing, dark night on 24th December. The moon was out but its light was hidden by the clouds of dust and mud high in the air. The sounds that night were of men shouting, rounds of bullets and screeching shells. No man's land, in-between ours and the Fritz (German) trenches, was full of crouching shadows and black, scorched trees as we kept fighting for a little more ground. That seems to be what this war is about – just a bit of ground!

We had no chance to think about Christmas Day, but in-between the fighting, we hung candles on tree branches.

The next morning, 25th December, was oddly quiet. The Germans had also hung candles and they had put trimmings, cut from scraps, on a little fir tree.

It was a misty Christmas morning and we were up to our knees in mud in our freezing dug-outs. We had parcels from loved ones and the Red Cross and we split the gifts between us. I got a pair of thick, woollen socks!

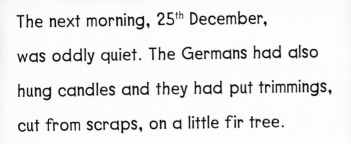

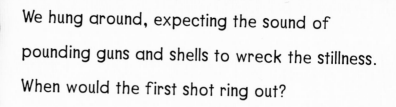

We hung around, expecting the sound of pounding guns and shells to wreck the stillness. When would the first shot ring out?

Well, it wasn't a shot that rung out but the sound of German soldiers singing Christmas carols!

We found ourselves stepping into no man's land to meet with the German soldiers. We shook hands and passed round food and drink with the men we had been ordered to kill.

Then it happened. Someone found a football! Without fuss, we formed teams. Worn out from weeks of fighting, we still found the strength to play on the frozen ground. No ref. Just helmets for goals. We slipped and skidded about in our big, muddy boots, and I tackled a German and kicked the ball to score! The Germans played well too. In the end, it was 3–2 to them, but we were *all* men and players to be proud of.

The true spirit of Christmas was in that truce and I'll be proud to tell my own children about it one day.

Well, the candle has gone out and I must sleep. Tell Mother I missed her Christmas cooking.

Your son,

Alfred

Troy Tomato
cooks up a storm

Would you employ this man as a chef?
He can hardly boil an egg!

In the TV kitchen

Today, Joy Floyd meets the well-known
chef Troy Tomato, and chats to him
as he cooks.

Joy: Good morning from the TV kitchen!

In today's show, Troy is going to
show us how to cook some of his
top dishes.

You've been cooking since you
were a boy, haven't you, Troy?

Troy: Yes – my Uncle Roy had some
good tips, and my Auntie
Septic always told me to wash
my hands first. You won't be
disappointed today, Joy. I think
you'll enjoy my food.

Joy: What's your best dish?

Troy: I do corking chips.
And my boil-in-the-bag fish isn't bad.
But it's not all about posh nosh.
Let me show you.

Joy: Oh yes, that sounds delightful!

Troy: First, I'm going to cook chicken
and mash, and pancakes.

Peel the spuds – ouch, try not to
peel your fingers – and boil them in
a pan (the spuds, not your fingers).

Put some foil on top of the chicken,
and put it in the oven.

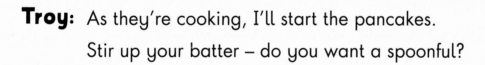

Troy: As they're cooking, I'll start the pancakes.
Stir up your batter – do you want a spoonful?

Joy: Er, no, thanks. It looks a bit lumpy.

Troy: Then swirl the oil in a non-stick pan.
When it's hot, tip in some batter –
and let it cook.
Then – toss!

Joy: The pancake's stuck
to the roof, Troy.

Troy: That's okay – I'll just
cook some more …

Joy: What was that noise – oh, no – it's the oven! You left the chicken in for too long, and it's blown up!

Troy: Oops! Next, mash the spuds – and squirt lots of ketchup on the top …

Joy: Look at my dress, Troy! I'm getting a bit annoyed!

Troy: Sorry! Well, the chicken is spoiled.

Joy: So is my best silk dress!

Troy: Let's try a boiled egg. I can't spoil a boiled egg, can I? Boil your water for about 3 mins – it's not boiling yet so I'll do a crab salad. Pick up your crab, like so – ouch! My finger! I forgot – first, kill your crab!

Joy: What's that hissing noise, Troy?

Troy: It's the water! Slight hitch – it's all boiled away – and I forgot to put the egg in! No boiled egg, then. Next, I'm going to cook fish with garlic and chilli. Mix up some garlic and chilli, and test it by putting a bit in your mouth – ouch! Aaargh! I forgot – chilli is hot!

Troy: Rub the garlic and chilli into the fish. Tip some oil into a pan, and add the fish. Cook it on the ring until it's golden, and then put it in the oven. Oh, no – I forgot – I've blown the oven up, haven't I? Well …

Joy: Troy, you've put too much oil in the pan! It's on fire! Quick! Put it out! Don't just flap a cloth at it! Stop the cameras …

You've destroyed the set, you fool! Our fantastic TV kitchen is a mess!

Troy: I'm sorry, Joy. I think I'll just stick to cooking fish and chips. Well, let's forget the chips.

Joy: And the fish!

Troy: Oh, I almost forgot. Can I sell you my cookbook? It's called "Troy Tomato Cooks Up a Storm". It's chock full of top tips, and it's just £75.99 …

Joy: Grrr … oh, what's the point? I quit!

Unwrap - and enjoy!

Listen up! Shout if you enjoy chocolate!

Lots of voices … OK, that's all of you! But what do you know about this scrummy snack?

The story of chocolate

Chocolate comes from cocoa beans grown in very hot parts of West Africa and South America. Long ago, the Mayas from South Mexico used the beans as cash, swapping them for other objects. Then they started to boil the beans and drink the liquid. The Aztecs followed the Mayas, and they called this liquid 'xocolatl' (or 'tchocolatl') – bitter water. The spoilt King Montezuma drank it from a gold cup!

Then in 1519, the Spanish explorer, Cortes, went to Mexico and found – chocolate!

In 1657, chocolate houses started opening in London, serving chocolate mixed with water or milk. They were very popular. Chocolate was here to stay!

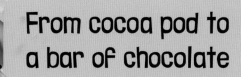

From cocoa pod to a bar of chocolate

Pull off the foil, open your mouth – and enjoy! You won't be disappointed. But how did your chocolate bar get here?

First, the cocoa pods are harvested.

Then the pods are left out in the hot sun.

The rest happens in a noisy factory, and lots of staff are employed to do it. The beans are scooped out of the pods, which are destroyed. Then the beans are cooked and ground into a thick, dark liquid with a strong smell – in a good way!

The liquid is sweetened and milk may be added.

It is stirred until it is smooth. And there you have it – chocolate!

But how is this turned into chocolate bars and sweets?

There are 3 ways:

1. For solid bars, the liquid chocolate is tipped into trays and cooled.

2. For filled bars, the hard fillings are set out on a conveyor belt and liquid chocolate is tipped over them. The filled bars are left to cool.

3. For chocolates with soft fillings or toys in them, the liquid is tipped into hollow pockets and cooled. Then the fillings are added and the bits are stuck together with chocolate.

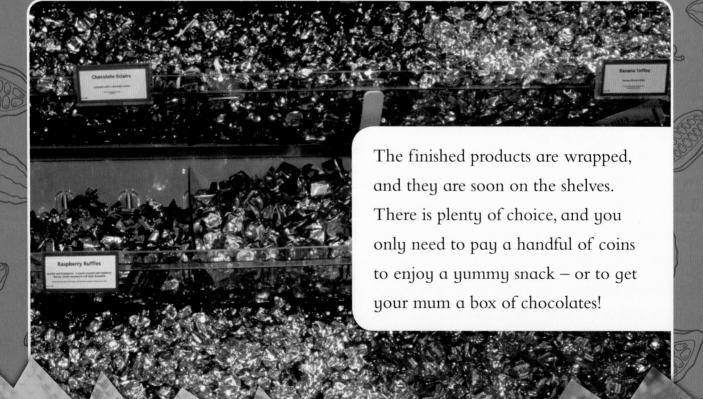

The finished products are wrapped, and they are soon on the shelves. There is plenty of choice, and you only need to pay a handful of coins to enjoy a yummy snack – or to get your mum a box of chocolates!

Did you know that...

- The first bar of chocolate was formed by Fry's in 1847.

- The largest bar of chocolate was formed in the UK in 2011 – it was a massive 6 tonnes!

- Dark chocolate is the king of chocolate – and a small helping is good for us!

- You need about 80 cocoa beans for just one 100 gram chocolate bar.

- This will annoy your pooch, but chocolate is poisonous to dogs – avoid feeding it to them!

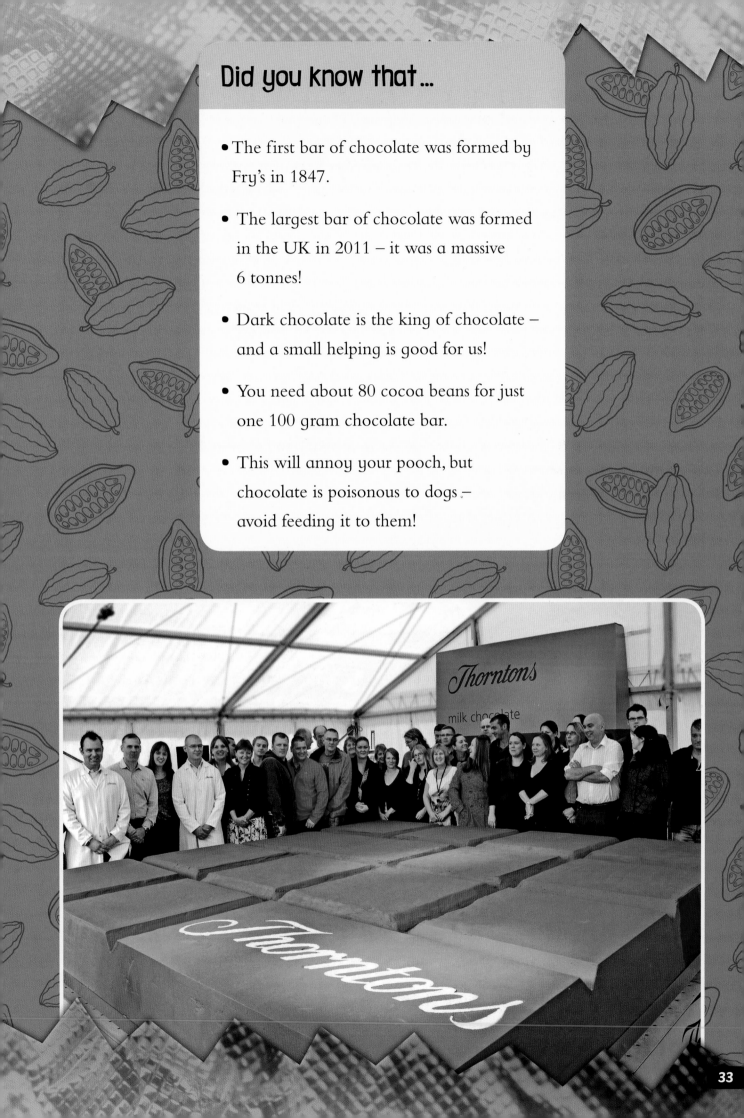

Room rage!

Can't find your black T-shirt?

Can't face going into your messy room?

Is it in a bit of a state?

Does your mum go on about it, and say,

"This room is like a rubbish tip!"

Are you a victim of ... **room rage?**

All teenage kids are the same – male and female!
But you can make your room a cool place to chill out
with your mates. Don't blame your mum – it's your job!
It's never too late to change your ways.

Get it sorted!

1. First, pick up all the rubbish on the floor.
(Is that a bit of Sunday's pizza under the
chair?) Throw it into a bin bag. Don't forget
to be green – save and recycle if you can.
It's not cheesy – it's to save the planet!

2. Take out all the dirty mugs and plates. Yes, and check under the bed. Bin that bit of stale cake left over from your last birthday party!

3. Pick up all the dirty socks and put them in the washing basket. Put a peg on your nose if you need to!

4. Hang up your shirts and put away your trackie bottoms. T-shirts, pants and socks go on a shelf, not on the floor, or the chair, or the lampshade!

5. Collect all the footie boots, laces and skates and put them in a corner. Important: skates left on the stairs are a no-no.

6. Vacuum the carpet – it's that noisy electric thing that sucks up dirt! Your mum will be impressed!

7. Shake out your sheets and pillowcases, and make the bed. It will feel good when you wake up in the morning. (Get rid of all the pet hairs and fluff. Don't let your Great Dane sleep on the bed – or your 10 long-haired cats!)

8. Put your books in the bookcase or on the shelf. You can fix any loose pages with sticky tape. If it's a good story, it helps if you can see the ending!

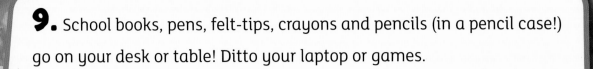

9. School books, pens, felt-tips, crayons and pencils (in a pencil case!) go on your desk or table! Ditto your laptop or games.

10. You may have toys, model planes, spaceships, games etc. that you have grown out of. Put them in a bag, so you can take them to a car boot sale. You may make lots of cash!

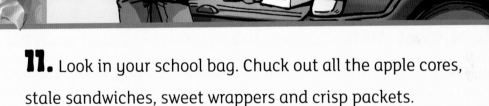

11. Look in your school bag. Chuck out all the apple cores, stale sandwiches, sweet wrappers and crisp packets.

12. Put your hairbrush, hair gel, stuff for spots, etc. in the bathroom. But watch out for your big brother – he may try to nick them when you're not looking!

13. Think about the walls. If your posters are flapping about, fix them with sticky-tack. Maybe you can get some fresh ones with cars on, or sports, or pop stars and bands. Ask if you can have a cork pinboard, so you can pin up photos, postcards, art and other cool stuff.

14. Last of all, put your name on the door: "Jake's room – knock before you come in!" (You should make your family knock so you can prepare them for the shock of seeing your room so tidy!)

Now you can enjoy your cool bedroom!

But don't forget – no more stale sandwiches, stinky socks and sticky bits of fluff. Give your room a tidy every week, and then you can have your mates round and you can get it all messy again!

Get your skates on!

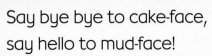

Lairy hair (air)

Green words: *Say the sounds. Say the word.*

h<u>air</u>   <u>air</u>   fl<u>air</u>   <u>ch</u><u>air</u>   f<u>air</u>   l<u>air</u>y   extra<u>or</u>din<u>air</u>e

Say the syllables. Say the word.

des|p<u>air</u>

Say the root word. Say the whole word.

rep<u>air</u> → rep<u>air</u>ing

Red words: s<u>ome</u>   d<u>oes</u>   <u>are</u>   <u>the</u>ir   <u>they</u>   <u>there</u>   <u>wh</u>at   <u>wh</u>ere   ca<u>ll</u>ed   a<u>ll</u>
c<u>ou</u>ld   was   want

Challenge words: custom<u>er</u>   mon<u>ey</u>   fa<u>sh</u>ion   wa<u>sh</u>   biza<u>rr</u>e   f<u>oo</u>tball   nu<u>mb</u><u>er</u>
tis<u>s</u>ue   try   w<u>eigh</u>t   hold   r<u>oa</u>ch   n<u>ow</u>   ev<u>er</u>y   h<u>air</u>dress <u>er</u>   m<u>ore</u>

Vocabulary check: lairy *flashy or behaving outrageously*   **barnet** *slang word for hair*

extraordinaire *excellent or outstanding*   **bizarre** *very strange and weird*

bliss *a state of joy*

Mrs Fairborn's baby (air)

Green words: *Say the sounds. Say the word.*

h<u>air</u>   <u>ch</u><u>air</u>   <u>air</u>   fl<u>air</u>

Say the syllables. Say the word.

F<u>air</u>|born   Al|is|t<u>air</u>   des|p<u>air</u>   f<u>air</u>|ly   un|f<u>air</u>   f<u>air</u>|y

Red words: s<u>ai</u>d   <u>one</u>   was   <u>wh</u>at   <u>wh</u>o   <u>are</u>   some   want   a<u>ll</u>   lo<u>ve</u>

Challenge words: baby   golden   wa<u>sh</u>   <u>ch</u>ild   bony   ev<u>er</u>
pronto   pr<u>air</u>ie   f<u>ol</u>k   Goldilo<u>ck</u>s   lady   beca<u>u</u><u>se</u>   most
even   h<u>air</u>dress <u>er</u>s   old   h<u>er</u>   h<u>air</u>do   f<u>ew</u>   <u>ou</u>t

Vocabulary check: tresses *long hair*   **adored** *loved*   **despair** *lose hope*

pronto *immediately*   **prairie dog** *a rodent, usually found in North America*

wizened *dried up*   **hectic** *busy*   **flair** *talent*

What sort of football fan are you? (ir)

Green words: *Say the sounds. Say the word.*

wh<u>ir</u>l   tw<u>ir</u>l   f<u>ir</u>st   f<u>ir</u>m   sm<u>ir</u>k

Say the syllables. Say the word.

d<u>ir</u>|ty   <u>th</u><u>irs</u>|ty

Say the root word. Say the whole word.

st<u>ir</u> → st<u>irr</u><u>ed</u>   pl<u>ay</u> → pl<u>ay</u>ing → pl<u>ay</u>ed

---

Red words: <u>wh</u>at   <u>are</u>   <u>wh</u>o   <u>th</u>ey   <u>th</u>ere   <u>on</u>e   ball

---

Challenge words: w<u>or</u>ld   s<u>ou</u>nds   dr<u>aw</u>   most   nose   post   try

g<u>oa</u>l   <u>wh</u>i<u>st</u>le   <u>ear</u>s   pl<u>ay</u> er   <u>ou</u>t   t<u>ea</u>ms   w<u>inn</u> er   gold   ref<u>er</u> <u>ee</u>

Vocabulary check: **fanatical** *a big fan*   **smirk** *a small smile*

It's football – but not as we know it! (ir)

Green words: *Say the sounds. Say the word.*

f<u>ir</u>st   f<u>ir</u>m   <u>sh</u><u>ir</u>t   st<u>ir</u>

Say the syllables. Say the word.

<u>th</u><u>ir</u>st|y   <u>th</u><u>ir</u>t|y   St<u>ir</u>|ling

Say the root word. Say the whole word.

d<u>ir</u>t → d<u>ir</u>ty   tw<u>ir</u>l → tw<u>ir</u>ling

Red words: <u>th</u>ey   <u>on</u>e   o<u>th</u> er   <u>are</u>   some   <u>wh</u>at   <u>th</u><u>eir</u>   w<u>ou</u>ld

w<u>er</u>e   ba<u>ll</u>   <u>tw</u>o   many   a<u>ll</u>

Challenge words: und<u>er</u><u>st</u>and   rules   diff<u>er</u>ent   <u>ea</u><u>ch</u>   c<u>ou</u>ntry   t<u>ea</u>m

h<u>al</u>ves   pl<u>ay</u>er   spikes   women   behind   g<u>oa</u>l   <u>ch</u>ange   names

col<u>our</u>   like   <u>wh</u>y   h<u>ow</u>   rubb er   holdin<u>g</u>   even

---

Vocabulary check: **crossbar** *horizontal bar between two upright posts of a goal*

Norman Knight, time-travelling superstar (ou)

Green words: *Say the sounds. Say the word.*

<u>ou</u>t   p<u>ou</u>nces   pr<u>ou</u>d   f<u>ou</u>l   gr<u>ou</u>nd   r<u>ou</u>nd   s<u>ou</u>nd   d<u>ou</u>bt

Say the syllables. Say the word.

th<u>ou</u>|sand   ab|<u>ou</u>t

Say the root word. Say the whole word.

b<u>ou</u>nce ➔ b<u>ou</u>ncing   ast<u>ou</u>nd ➔ ast<u>ou</u>nding

Red words: <u>th</u>ere   what   come   won   <u>th</u>eir   one   ba<u>ll</u>

Challenge words: d<u>ow</u>n   n<u>ow</u>   only   save   take   time   moments   game

super<u>star</u>   g<u>oa</u>lie   try<u>ing</u>

Vocabulary check: **spuds** *potatoes*   **stacks** *lots of*   **tash** *moustache*   **slick** *smooth*

Christmas 1914 (ou)

Green words: *Say the sounds. Say the word.*

<u>ou</u>r   h<u>ou</u><u>se</u>   pr<u>ou</u>d   <u>ou</u>t   cl<u>ou</u>ds   s<u>ou</u>nds   r<u>ou</u>nds   gr<u>ou</u>nd   f<u>ou</u>nd

Say the syllables. Say the word.

acc|<u>ou</u>nt   a|r<u>ou</u>nd

Say the root word. Say the whole word.

<u>sh</u><u>ou</u>t ➔ <u>sh</u><u>ou</u>ting   cr<u>ou</u><u>ch</u> ➔ cr<u>ou</u><u>ch</u>ing   p<u>ou</u>nd ➔ p<u>ou</u>nding

Red words: was   <u>th</u>ey   were   who   <u>th</u>ere   Fa<u>th</u>er   son   co<u>u</u>ld   Mo<u>th</u>er   <u>sh</u><u>ou</u>ld   want   what   on<u>es</u>   would   a<u>ll</u>   loved

Challenge words: Brit<u>ai</u>n   w<u>ar</u>   Germany   f<u>ough</u>t   lett<u>er</u>   Decemb<u>er</u>   d<u>ear</u>est   sold<u>ier</u>   cold   <u>or</u>d<u>er</u>ed   teams   g<u>oa</u>ls   play<u>er</u>s   tr<u>ue</u>   truce   old   England   som<u>eone</u>   frozen

Vocabulary check: **trenches** *deep ditches where soldiers lived in the First World War*

Tommy *English soldier*   **shells** *missiles containing explosives*   **Red Cross** *a charity*

pounding *hammering, thumping sounds*   **truce** *an agreement not to fight*

Troy Tomato cooks up a storm (oy oi)

Green words: *Say the sounds. Say the word.*

Joy   foil   Troy   oil   boil   boy   Roy

Say the syllables. Say the word.

en|joy

Say the root word. Say the whole word.

spoil → spoiled   disappoint → disappointed

Red words: would   some   were   what   all   want   was   call

Challenge words: Tomato   chef   how   Auntie   told   always
wash   won't   try   pancakes   like   water   golden   oven
fire   almost   fingers   batter

Vocabulary check: **employ** *to give a job to somebody*   **bangers** *sausages*   **corking** *excellent*
nosh *food*   **hitch** *problem*   **chock full** *jammed full*

Unwrap – and enjoy! (oy oi)

Green words: *Say the sounds. Say the word.*

voi ces   boil   foil   toys   ch oi ce   coins

Say the syllables. Say the word.

en|joy   noi|sy   ann|oy   a|void

Say the root word. Say the whole word.

disappoint → disappointed   employ → employed   destroy → destroyed

Red words: all   what   comes   other   they   water   was   here   are
there   small

Challenge words: chocolate   cocoa   beans   Mexico   swapping   bitter
Montezuma   gold   explorer   opening   serving   turned   conveyor   together
only   Fry's   tonnes   poisonous   listen   used   London   popular   how   over

Vocabulary check: **harvested** *to pick crops*   **ground** *crushed into small pieces*

Room rage! (a–e)

Green words: *Say the sounds. Say the word.*

face state rage male same make blame place wake Jake stale

Say the syllables. Say the word.

birth|day lamp|shade book|case

Red words: are all any should does watch ones other Great

Challenge words: pinboard photos now prepare tidy try find recycle washing nose vacuum trackie female like never under over corner wrapp ers walls posters postcard every

Vocabulary check: ditto *the same*   **stale** *not fresh*

Get your skates on! (a–e)

Green words: *Say the sounds. Say the word.*

skates Jake wake late Tate cake plate Grace face
Kate game mate save state race brake

Say the syllables. Say the word.

corn|flakes mis|take

Red words: what

Challenge words: means bye every skateboard never down why hi hello wow

Vocabulary check: state *mess, dirty or untidy*